HERSHEY'S

Contents

KISSES Peanut Butter Blossoms

MAKES ABOUT 48 COOKIES

48 HERSHEY'S KISSES Milk Chocolates

¾ cup REESE'S Creamy Peanut Butter

½ cup shortening

⅓ cup granulated sugar

⅓ cup packed light brown sugar

1 egg

2 tablespoons milk

1 teaspoon vanilla extract

1½ cups all-purpose flour

1 teaspoon baking soda

½ teaspoon salt

⅓ cup additional granulated sugar for rolling

1. Heat oven to 375°F. Remove wrappers from chocolates.

2. Beat peanut butter and shortening with mixer on medium speed in large bowl until well blended. Add ⅓ cup granulated sugar and brown sugar; beat until fluffy. Add egg, milk and vanilla; beat well. Stir together flour, baking soda and salt; gradually beat into peanut butter mixture.

3. Shape dough into 1-inch balls. Roll in additional granulated sugar; place on ungreased cookie sheet.

4. Bake 8 to 10 minutes or until lightly browned. Immediately press a chocolate into center of each cookie; cookies will crack around edges. Remove to wire racks and cool completely. ■

White & Chocolate Covered Strawberries

MAKES ABOUT 3 DOZEN BERRIES

2 cups (12-ounce package) HERSHEY'S Kitchens Premier White Chips

2 tablespoons shortening (do not use butter, margarine, spread or oil), divided

4 cups (2 pints) fresh strawberries, rinsed, patted dry and chilled

1 cup HERSHEY'S Kitchens SPECIAL DARK Chocolate Chips or HERSHEY'S Kitchens Semi-Sweet Chocolate Chips

1. Cover tray with wax paper.

2. Place white chips and 1 tablespoon shortening in medium microwave-safe bowl. Microwave at MEDIUM (50%) 1 minute; stir until chips are melted and mixture is smooth. If necessary, microwave at MEDIUM an additional 15 seconds at a time, just until smooth when stirred.

3. Holding by top, dip one third of each strawberry into white chip mixture; shake gently to remove excess. Place on prepared tray; refrigerate until coating is firm, at least 30 minutes.

4. Repeat microwave procedure with chocolate chips and remaining shortening in clean microwave-safe bowl. Dip lower one third of each berry into chocolate mixture. Refrigerate until firm. Cover; refrigerate leftover strawberries. ■

REESE'S Peanut Butter Bark

MAKES ABOUT 1 POUND CANDY

2 packages (4 ounces each) HERSHEY'S Kitchens Semi-Sweet Chocolate Baking Bars, broken into pieces

1⅔ cups (10-ounce package) REESE'S Peanut Butter Chips

1 tablespoon shortening (do not use butter, margarine, spread or oil)

½ cup roasted peanuts or toasted almonds,* coarsely chopped

*To toast almonds: Heat oven to 350°F. Spread almonds in thin layer in shallow baking pan. Bake 8 to 10 minutes, stirring occasionally, until light golden brown; cool.

1. Cover tray with wax paper.

2. Place chocolate in medium microwave-safe bowl. Microwave at MEDIUM (50%) 1 minute; stir. If necessary, microwave at MEDIUM an additional 15 seconds at a time, stirring after each heating, until chocolate is melted and smooth when stirred.

3. Immediately place peanut butter chips and shortening in second microwave-safe bowl. Microwave at MEDIUM 1 minute; stir. If necessary, microwave at MEDIUM an additional 15 seconds at a time, stirring after each heating, until chips are melted and mixture is smooth when stirred; stir in peanuts.

4. Alternately spoon above mixtures onto prepared tray; swirl with knife for marbled effect. Gently tap tray on countertop to even thickness of mixture. Cover; refrigerate until firm. Break into pieces. Store in cool, dry place. ■

Rich Cocoa Crinkle Cookies

MAKES ABOUT 6 DOZEN COOKIES

2 cups granulated sugar
¾ cup vegetable oil
1 cup HERSHEY'S Cocoa
4 eggs
2 teaspoons vanilla extract
2⅓ cups all-purpose flour
2 teaspoons baking powder
½ teaspoon salt
Powdered sugar for rolling

1. Combine granulated sugar and oil in large bowl; add cocoa, beating until well blended. Beat in eggs and vanilla. Stir together flour, baking powder and salt. Gradually add to cocoa mixture, beating well.

2. Cover; refrigerate until dough is firm enough to handle, at least 6 hours.

3. Heat oven to 350°F. Line cookie sheet with parchment paper or lightly grease. Shape dough into 1-inch balls; roll in powdered sugar to coat. Place about 2 inches apart on prepared cookie sheet.

4. Bake 10 to 12 minutes or until almost no indentation remains when touched lightly and tops are crackled. Cool slightly. Remove from cookie sheet to wire rack. Cool completely. ■

HERSHEY'S SPECIAL DARK Chocolate Layered Cheesecake

MAKES 12 SERVINGS

CHOCOLATE CRUMB CRUST (recipe follows)

3 packages (8 ounces each) cream cheese, softened

¾ cup sugar

4 eggs

¼ cup heavy cream

2 teaspoons vanilla extract

¼ teaspoon salt

2 cups (12-ounce package) HERSHEY'S Kitchens SPECIAL DARK Chocolate Chips, divided

½ teaspoon shortening (do not use butter, margarine, spread or oil)

1. Prepare CHOCOLATE CRUMB CRUST. Heat oven to 350°F.

2. Beat cream cheese and sugar in large bowl until smooth. Gradually beat in eggs, heavy cream, vanilla and salt, beating until well blended; set aside.

3. Set aside 2 tablespoons chocolate chips. Place remaining chips in large microwave-safe bowl. Microwave at MEDIUM (50%) 1½ minutes; stir. If necessary, microwave at MEDIUM an additional 15 seconds at a time, stirring after each heating, until chocolate is melted when stirred.

4. Gradually blend 1½ cups cheesecake batter into melted chocolate. Spread 2 cups chocolate mixture in prepared crust.

5. Blend another 2 cups plain cheesecake batter into remaining chocolate mixture; spread 2 cups of this mixture over first layer. Stir remaining cheesecake batter into remaining chocolate mixture; spread over second layer.

6. Bake 50 to 55 minutes or until center is almost set. Remove from oven to wire rack. With knife, immediately loosen cake from side of pan. Cool to room temperature.

7. Place reserved chocolate chips and shortening in small microwave-safe bowl. Microwave at MEDIUM 30 seconds; stir. If necessary, microwave at MEDIUM an additional 10 seconds at a time, stirring after each heating, until chocolate is melted and smooth when stirred. Drizzle over top of cheesecake. Cover; refrigerate several hours until cold. Cover and refrigerate leftover cheesecake.

Chocolate Crumb Crust: Stir together 1½ cups vanilla wafer crumbs (about 45 wafers, crushed), ½ cup powdered sugar and ¼ cup HERSHEY'S Cocoa; stir in ¼ cup (½ stick) melted butter or margarine. Press mixture onto bottom and 1½ inches up sides of 9-inch springform pan. ■

Secret KISSES Cookies

MAKES ABOUT 36 COOKIES

- 1 cup (2 sticks) butter or margarine, softened
- ½ cup granulated sugar
- 1 teaspoon vanilla extract
- 1¾ cups all-purpose flour
- 1 cup finely chopped walnuts or almonds
- 36 HERSHEY'S KISSES Milk Chocolates or HERSHEY'S KISSES Milk Chocolates with Almonds
- Powdered sugar for rolling

1. Beat butter, granulated sugar and vanilla with mixer on medium speed in large bowl until fluffy. Add flour and walnuts; beat on low speed of mixer until well blended. Cover; refrigerate 1 to 2 hours or until dough is firm enough to handle.

2. Remove wrappers from chocolates. Heat oven to 375°F. Using about 1 tablespoon dough for each cookie, shape dough around each chocolate; roll in hand to make ball. (Be sure to cover each chocolate piece completely.) Place on ungreased cookie sheet.

3. Bake 10 to 12 minutes or until cookies are set but not browned. Cool slightly; remove to wire rack. While still slightly warm, roll in powdered sugar. Cool completely. Store in tightly covered container. Roll again in powdered sugar just before serving.

Variation: Sift together 1 tablespoon HERSHEY'S Cocoa with ⅓ cup powdered sugar. Roll warm cookies in cocoa mixture. ■

REESE'S Peanut Butter & HERSHEY'S KISSES Pie

MAKES 8 SERVINGS

- About 42 HERSHEY'S KISSES Milk Chocolates, divided
- 2 tablespoons milk
- 1 packaged (8-inch) crumb crust (6 ounces)
- 1 package (8 ounces) cream cheese, softened
- ¾ cup sugar
- 1 cup REESE'S Creamy Peanut Butter
- 1 container (8 ounces) frozen non-dairy whipped topping, thawed and divided

1. Remove wrappers from chocolates. Place 26 chocolates and milk in small microwave-safe bowl. Microwave at MEDIUM (50%) 1 minute or just until melted and smooth when stirred. Spread evenly on bottom of crust. Refrigerate about 30 minutes.

2. Beat cream cheese with mixer on medium speed in medium bowl until smooth; gradually beat in sugar, then peanut butter, beating well after each addition. Reserve ½ cup whipped topping; fold remaining whipped topping into peanut butter mixture. Spoon into crust over chocolate. Cover; refrigerate about 6 hours or until set.

3. Garnish with reserved whipped topping and remaining chocolates. Cover; refrigerate leftover pie. ■

Crispy Chocolate Ice Cream Mud Pie

MAKES 8 SERVINGS

½ cup HERSHEY'S Syrup

⅓ cup HERSHEY'S Kitchens SPECIAL DARK Chocolate Chips or HERSHEY'S Kitchens Semi-Sweet Chocolate Chips

2 cups crisp rice cereal

4 cups (1 quart) vanilla ice cream, divided

4 cups (1 quart) chocolate ice cream, divided

Additional HERSHEY'S Syrup

1. Butter 9-inch pie plate.

2. Place ½ cup chocolate syrup and chocolate chips in medium microwave-safe bowl. Microwave at MEDIUM (50%) 45 seconds or until hot; stir until smooth. Reserve ¼ cup chocolate syrup mixture; set aside. Add cereal to remaining chocolate syrup mixture, stirring until well coated; cool slightly.

3. Press cereal mixture, using back of spoon, evenly on bottom and up side of prepared pie plate to form crust. Place in freezer 15 to 20 minutes or until crust is firm. Spread half of vanilla ice cream into crust; spoon reserved ¼ cup chocolate syrup mixture over layer. Spread half of chocolate ice cream over sauce.

4. Top with alternating scoops of vanilla and chocolate ice cream. Cover; return to freezer until serving time. Drizzle with additional chocolate syrup just before serving. ■

Peanut Butter Fudge Brownie Bars

MAKES ABOUT 24 BARS

- 1 cup (2 sticks) butter or margarine, melted
- 1½ cups sugar
- 2 eggs
- 1 teaspoon vanilla extract
- 1¼ cups all-purpose flour
- ⅔ cup HERSHEY'S Cocoa
- ¼ cup milk
- 1¼ cups chopped pecans or walnuts, divided
- ½ cup (1 stick) butter or margarine
- 1⅔ cups (10-ounce package) REESE'S Peanut Butter Chips
- 1 can (14 ounces) sweetened condensed milk (not evaporated milk)
- ¼ cup HERSHEY'S Kitchens SPECIAL DARK Chocolate Chips or HERSHEY'S Kitchens Semi-Sweet Chocolate Chips

1. Heat oven to 350°F. Grease 13×9×2-inch baking pan.

2. Beat melted butter, sugar, eggs and vanilla in large bowl with mixer on medium speed until well blended. Add flour, cocoa and milk; beat until blended. Stir in 1 cup nuts. Spread in prepared pan.

3. Bake 25 to 30 minutes or just until edges begin to pull away from sides of pan. Cool completely in pan on wire rack.

4. Melt ½ cup butter and peanut butter chips in medium saucepan over low heat, stirring constantly. Add sweetened condensed milk, stirring until smooth; pour over baked layer.

5. Place chocolate chips in small microwave-safe bowl. Microwave at MEDIUM (50%) 45 seconds or just until chips are melted when stirred. Drizzle bars with melted chocolate; sprinkle with remaining ¼ cup nuts. Refrigerate 1 hour or until firm. Cut into bars. Cover; refrigerate leftover bars. ■

Classic Chocolate Cream Pie

MAKES 8 SERVINGS

- 5 sections (½ ounce each) HERSHEY'S Kitchens Unsweetened Chocolate Baking Bar, broken into pieces
- 3 cups milk, divided
- 1⅓ cups sugar
- 3 tablespoons all-purpose flour
- 3 tablespoons cornstarch
- ½ teaspoon salt
- 3 egg yolks
- 2 tablespoons butter or margarine
- 1½ teaspoons vanilla extract
- 1 baked (9-inch) pie crust, cooled, or 1 (9-inch) crumb crust
- Sweetened whipped cream (optional)

1. Combine chocolate and 2 cups milk in medium saucepan; cook over medium heat, stirring constantly, just until mixture boils. Remove from heat and set aside.

2. Stir together sugar, flour, cornstarch and salt in medium bowl. Whisk remaining 1 cup milk into egg yolks in separate bowl; stir into sugar mixture. Gradually add to chocolate mixture. Cook over medium heat, whisking constantly, until mixture boils; boil and stir 1 minute. Remove from heat; stir in butter and vanilla.

3. Pour into prepared crust; press plastic wrap directly onto surface. Cool; refrigerate until well chilled. Top with whipped cream, if desired. ■

Chocolate Streusel Bars

MAKES ABOUT 24 BARS

1¾ cups all-purpose flour

1 cup sugar

¼ cup HERSHEY'S Cocoa

½ cup (1 stick) butter or margarine

1 egg

1 can (14 ounces) sweetened condensed milk (not evaporated milk)

2 cups (12-ounce package) HERSHEY'S Kitchens SPECIAL DARK Chocolate Chips or HERSHEY'S Kitchens Semi-Sweet Chocolate Chips, divided

1 cup coarsely chopped nuts

1. Heat oven to 350°F. Grease 13×9×2-inch baking pan.

2. Stir together flour, sugar and cocoa in large bowl. Cut in butter until mixture resembles coarse crumbs. Add egg; mix well. Set aside 1½ cups mixture. Press remaining mixture onto bottom of prepared pan. Bake crust 10 minutes.

3. Meanwhile, place sweetened condensed milk and 1 cup chocolate chips in medium microwave-safe bowl; stir. Microwave at MEDIUM (50%) 1 to 1½ minutes or until chips are melted and mixture is smooth when stirred; pour over crust. Add nuts and remaining chips to reserved crumb mixture. Sprinkle over top.

4. Bake an additional 25 to 30 minutes or until center is almost set. Cool completely in pan on wire rack. Cut into bars. ■

Chocolate Magic Mousse Pie

MAKES 8 SERVINGS

- 1 envelope unflavored gelatin
- 2 tablespoons cold water
- ¼ cup boiling water
- 1 cup sugar
- ½ cup HERSHEY'S Cocoa
- 2 cups (1 pint) cold whipping cream
- 2 teaspoons vanilla extract
- 1 packaged (8-inch) graham cracker crumb crust (6 ounces)
- Refrigerated light whipped cream in pressurized can or frozen whipped topping, thawed

1. Sprinkle gelatin over cold water in small bowl; let stand 2 minutes to soften. Add boiling water; stir until gelatin is completely dissolved and mixture is clear. Cool slightly.

2. Mix sugar and cocoa in large bowl; add whipping cream and vanilla. Beat on medium speed, scraping bottom of bowl often, until mixture is stiff. Pour in gelatin mixture; beat until well blended.

3. Spoon into crust. Refrigerate about 3 hours. Top with whipped cream and garnish as desired. Cover; store leftover pie in refrigerator. ■

English Toffee Bars

MAKES ABOUT 24 BARS

- 2 cups all-purpose flour
- 1 cup packed light brown sugar
- ½ cup (1 stick) cold butter
- 1 cup pecan halves
- TOFFEE TOPPING (recipe follows)
- 1 cup HERSHEY'S Kitchens Milk Chocolate Chips

1. Heat oven to 350°F.

2. Combine flour and brown sugar in large bowl. With pastry blender or fork, cut in butter until fine crumbs form (a few large crumbs may remain). Press mixture onto bottom of ungreased 13×9×2-inch baking pan. Sprinkle pecans over crust. Prepare TOFFEE TOPPING; drizzle evenly over pecans and crust.

3. Bake 20 to 22 minutes or until topping is bubbly and golden; remove from oven. Immediately sprinkle milk chocolate chips evenly over top; press gently onto surface. Cool completely in pan on wire rack. Cut into bars.

Toffee Topping: Combine ⅔ cup butter and ⅓ cup packed light brown sugar in small saucepan; cook over medium heat, stirring constantly, until mixture comes to a boil. Continue boiling, stirring constantly, 30 seconds. Use immediately. ■

Chocolate Syrup Swirl Cake

MAKES 12 SERVINGS

- 1 cup (2 sticks) butter or margarine, softened
- 2 cups sugar
- 2 teaspoons vanilla extract
- 3 eggs
- 2¾ cups all-purpose flour
- 1¼ teaspoons baking soda, divided
- ½ teaspoon salt
- 1 cup buttermilk or sour milk*
- 1 cup HERSHEY'S Syrup
- 1 cup sweetened coconut flakes (optional)

*To sour milk: Use 1 tablespoon white vinegar plus milk to equal 1 cup.

1. Heat oven to 350°F. Grease and flour 12-cup fluted tube pan or 10-inch tube pan.

2. Beat butter, sugar and vanilla in large bowl until fluffy. Add eggs; beat well. Stir together flour, 1 teaspoon baking soda and salt; add alternately with buttermilk to butter mixture, beating until well blended.

3. Measure 2 cups batter in small bowl; stir in syrup and remaining ¼ teaspoon baking soda. Add coconut, if desired, to remaining vanilla batter; pour into prepared pan. Pour chocolate batter over vanilla batter in pan; do not mix.

4. Bake 60 to 70 minutes or until wooden pick inserted in center comes out clean. Cool 15 minutes; remove from pan to wire rack. Cool completely; glaze or frost as desired. ■